T0088907

Takumbeng & Other Poems from the Grassfields in Cameroon

Peter Wuteh Vakunta

Langaa Research & Publishing CIG
Mankon, Bamenda

Publisher:

Langaa RPCIG
Langaa Research & Publishing Common Initiative Group
P.O. Box 902 Mankon
Bamenda
North West Region
Cameroon
Langaagrp@gmail.com
www.langaa-rpcig.net

Distributed in and outside N. America by African Books Collective
orders@africanbookscollective.com
www.africanbookscollective.com

ISBN: 9956-762-40-7

DISCLAIMER
All views expressed in this publication are those of the author and do
not necessarily reflect the views of Langaa RPCIG.

Dedication

To the fallen heroes of Abakwa

Table of Contents

Preface

Takumbeng and Other Poems from Abakwa is a tribute to the Takumbeng in Cameroon. The *Takumbeng*, a female secret society in the Northwest Region, has played a critical role in changing the political landscape of Cameroon. The militancy of this group has empowered rural and urban women in their strife to ensure democratic governance and human rights protection under the regime of Paul Biya. It should be noted that *Takumbeng* has been in existence since the pre-colonial era but they came into the limelight in the 1990s in the wake of political liberalization in Cameroon that ushered in a new dispensation, following the launch of the Social Democratic Front (SDF) on May 26, 1990. The group derives its name from the society of Princes in the Bafut fondom (Fonchingong and Tanga, 2007) but its members hail from the fondoms of Akum, Bafut, Bambui, Bambili, Kedjom Keku, Kedjom Ketinguh, Mendankwe, Chomba, Nkwen, and Santa. The strength of the *Takumbeng* resides in its numerical value and mobilization for the course of social justice. They became prominent at the time of Cameroon's uneasy transition from unitary to multiparty politics in the early 90s (Takougang & Kieger, 1998).

There is no gainsaying the fact the *Takumbeng* and its precursors, the *Anlu and Fombwen* have contributed significantly to shaping the course of political activism in Cameroon. They have lent their voice to opposition parties' demands for political freedoms in the country. The role of the *Takumbeng* in matters of social cohesion cannot be underestimated. The group functions as agents of ritualistic cleansing, enjoining women to refrain from acts of deprecation such as adultery, alcoholism, witchcraft, and gossip. This secret society plays a role analogous to that played by male secret societies in the Grassfields in Cameroon such as *Kwifon, Tifuan, Nwo* and *Ngwerung*. *Takumbeng* uses occult powers to check excesses in the community. Their modus operandi of using nudity to cast aspersions on evildoers has been transformed into a powerful tool now used by these women to press for political freedoms in Cameroon. Kah (2011) observes that "The display of nakedness of the African woman was and remains her expression of anger and outrage at both public injustice and private male viciousness" (73). The women make use of their bodies as a combat tool; stripping themselves naked when threatened by authority figures. This is based on the belief that an exposed vagina is an ill omen in the Grassfields of Cameroon. Kah (2011) notes that the symbolic power of the vagina was used by the *Takumbeng* to cow gun-toting soldiers in Bamenda into submission in the early 1990s following the re-introduction of multiparty politics in Cameroon. The militancy of the *Takumbeng* gained leverage during the Ghost Town operations or *Villes Mortes* in Cameroon initiated by opposition parties in a bid to force Paul Biya out of office. These women used their bodies as symbolic and metaphorical devices to subvert the dominant discourse of manipulation. The practice of undressing and exposing their nudity constitute their magic wand. Their approach is pacific.

In general, the Takumbeng are post-menopausal women believed to be immune to witchcraft, sorcery and effects of traditional medicine or *megan*. These women exercise considerable influence and are sometimes able to assume ritual roles that were, hitherto, denied them (Awasom, 2002). The most potent weapon of the *Takumbeng* is the ritual of uncovering their nakedness to anyone who attempts to resist their injunctions and actions. It must be underscored that during the current dispensation in Cameroon, the *Takumbeng* has metamorphosed from an indigenous secret society to a contemporary resistance group determined to put an end to political intransigence, abuse of human rights and economic deprivation. The political activism of the *Takumbeng* is comparable to the momentum gathered by the activities of other female resistance movements in Africa, such as the Aba riots of 1929 (Fonchingong and Tanga, 2007), the activities of Kenyan women involved in the Mau Mau war of liberation (1952-1957), the Pare Women's resistance in Tanzania (Feierman, 1990) and the protest movement of women in the Niger Delta region of Nigeria who have been fighting for compensation from oil companies. The collective resolve of the *Takumbeng* and unbendable commitment to social justice are indelible legacies that Cameroon owes this group of valiant women. The transformation of the *Takumbeng* from the status of a secret society to that of resistance movement has yielded dividends for opposition parties in Cameroon given the unalloyed support that this group has lent to proponents of democratic governance in Cameroon such as the SDF. The militancy of the *Takumbeng* has paved the way for socially responsible governance. Their actions have engendered a culture of social protest and political consciousness. Their actions check the excesses of administrators in Cameroon (Fonchingong and Tanga, 2007).

In sum, the militancy of the *Takumbeng* has had economic, cultural, social and political ramifications for the New Deal in Cameroon. During the pro-democracy movement in Cameroon, the *Takumbeng* showed proof of women's leadership capabilities by playing a multitude of roles—mobilization and raising awareness of the public through civil disobedience campaigns, lampooning acts of injustice through demonstrations, educating the public on questions of human rights violations, monitoring the voting process and fostering free and fair election processes. In this light, this collection of poems is intended to be a celebration of the prowess of the *Takembeng*. Not all the poems in the collection pertain to the *Takumbeng* but even those that do not relate to the secret society address human rights violations and other forms of societal ills that constitute the plague of contemporary society. It is written in impeccable Standard English. The strength of the book resides in the vastness of the thematic terrain broached. It is a treasure trove of knowledge that would nourish every avid soul.

Indigenous Mores

Tribute to Takumbeng

Takumbeng,
Women of steel; women of valor,
Fire-spitting females unfazed by Mbiayaism [1],
You refuse to be cowed into submission
By the gestapo of LRC [2]

Takumbeng,
Female dare-devils
In whose unyielding hands
Scatology and nudity serve as lethal ammo
Against emasculators of social justice.

Takumbeng,
Women of age, women of candor,
When the hawks came after Titabet [3]
You stood hands akimbo and refused
To budge in the face of intimidation, beatings and rape.

Takumbeng,
Sorority of the post-menopausals,
Whose might astounded the world
In the 1990's in Abakwa during
The wee hours of demo-craziness in Ongola.

Takumbeng,
Backbone of the Social Democratic Front
Harbinger of political liberalism.
You stood firm when the SDF
Saw the light of day at Ntarikon on May 26.

Angered by the demise of six young Abakwans,
Unperturbed by the heavy handed attempts
To abort the event by forces from LRC,
You counter-attacked
With brimstone and venom.

True to yourselves,
You've remained the backbone
Of the opposition in Nooremac [4],
Stimulating militancy and adding beef
To the democratic bare bones in Ongola.

Takumbeng—a string of nomenclature—
Takembeng, Akeeken, Tamanjong—
Offspring of many fondoms in graffi land—
Bafut, Bambili, Kedjom Keku, Kedjom Ketinguh,
Mendankwe, Chomba, Mbatu, Nkwen, Santa.

Takumbeng— life-blood of womenfolk,
Entrusted with a myriad of duties—
Purification, exorcism, social justice,
Communalism, decision-making, mediation,
Cleansing, funeral rites, social pacification,
And communion with Kwifon.

Takumbeng,
A formidable force to reckon with—
Endowed with mystical prowess.
Avant-garde of the infamous *Villes Mortes*,[5]
Takumbeng lives in the hindsight of Abakwa citizenry.

Takumbeng,
Indefatigable women whose

4

Role in civil disobedience
Is no sinecure at all,
You block the flow of goods
And foodstuff to the cities.

Large blades of grass
In the mouth of the Takumbeng
Symbolise "no talk but action"
The *nkeng*, dracaena plant,
Symbol of peace in graffi land.

Another lethal weapon
In the hands of the Takumbeng,
Celebrated for nocturnal rituals,
Symbol of womanhood,
Incarnation of occultism.

Takumbeng,
Queens of the earth,
And architects of life,
By virtue of procreation,
Takumbeng is no trifling matter.

Takumbeng,
Indigenous secret society,
Metamorphosed into militant group.
To counter male chauvinism,
Abuse and misgovernment.

Takumbeng transcends ethnic frontiers.
Agents of ritualistic cleansing,
Nocturnal witchdoctors,
Purveyors of ominous signs,

You ensure social cohesion.

Takumbeng,
Your agenda includes rallying
Womenfolk for communal labor.
Your resolve to right
The wrongs of society is a creed.

Takumbeng's nudity far being
A sign of vulnerability,
Rather it's fortitude,
Queens of the earth.
Hail Takumbeng!

Takumbeng,
Architects of life.
Your resolve to protect humanity,
By virtue of womanhood,
Admirable affront aimed at evil-doers.

Even more laudable is your use of
Traditional symbolic rituals,
Mystic powers and shaming as combat tools.
Recourse to symbolism
Being extra ammunition to your stock in trade.

The exposed vagina,
Harbinger of ill-omen,
The exposed bare breast,
One more lethal weapon,
The whistle a rallying call for war.

Awe-inspiring ululations,
Formidable bulwark against
Forces of oppression.
Bodies adorned with
Macabre paraphernalia—

Torn male dresses, dry banana leaves,
Fresh creeping plants, charcoal,
Wood ash and dry grass knots,
All tools of desecration
In the hands of *Takumbeng.*

Takumbeng take matters
Seriously when despised,
Performing mock burials,
That send cold shivers down the spines of victims
Who take to their heels Or drop dead!

Graffi

Graffi—
What's this lexeme?
What does it connote?
Nomenclature pregnant with meaning.

Graffi—
Corrosion of the onomastic
Label 'Grassfields'
Alias Grasslands of the Northwest Region.

Graffi—
Graffi people are legion;
Seven divisions; several tongues—
Boyo, Bui, Donga-Mantung…

That's far from finished—
Menchum, Mezam, Momo & Ngoketunjia.
Graffi Land, home of age-old secret societies—
Takembeng, Kwifon, Anlu, Kelu, Akeken, Tamanjong...

There's more—
Tifuan, Nwo, Nwerung and Fonbuen.
Formidable occult societies
Endowed with awe-inspiring prowess.

Graffi Land—
Home of virtuosos—
Bernard Nsokika Fonlon,
John Ngu Foncha

The list is long—
Solomon Tandeng Muna,
Augustine Ngom Jua
Albert Womah Mukong..

The count continues—
Nde Tumasah,
Simon Achidi Achu
Ni John Fru Ndi…

And still more—
Fonka Shang Lawrence,
Fon Gorji Dinka,
Daniel Noni Lantum…

Graffi Land—
Hot bed of political Opposition—
Social Democratic Front,
Kamerun National Congress.

Grassfields—
Cradle of revolutionary ideologies—
Ghost Town Operation,
Alias *Villes Mortes.*

Graffi Land—
Conglomerate of fondoms—
Kom, Nso, Bali,Mankon,
Bafut, Bali, Bu, Befang…

Grasslands—
Network of chiefdoms—
Bamunka, Babungo, Babessi,

Baba I, Bambalang, Nsei…

The list continues—
Babessi, Bafanji, Bamali,
Bali Gansing, Bangolan,
Balikumbat, Bali Gashu.

Graffi Land—
Home of martryrs,
Land where heroes go to die,
Land of 'come-no-go,' Abakwa![1]

---

[1] Bamenda

Ndobo (A Legend of Ndop)

From Tikari they came legion.
They came as one family,
A family of thirteen sons.
All sons of one woman.
They came in search
Of arable land to pitch camp.

But ere long,
Gripes and feuds put
The siblings at loggerheads.
And things fell apart!
In a bid to ward off bloodshed,
Brothers parted ways in peace.

Here then is the
Genesis of the thirteen villages
That make up the region known as Ndop—
Bamunka, Babungo, Babessi,
Baba I, Bambalang, Nsei…
In the Division of Ngo-Ketunjia.

The list continues—
Babessi, Bafanji, Bamali,
Bali Gansing, Bangolan,
Balimkumbat, Bali Gashu.
Legion has it that these villages
Earned the epithet 'Ba' from colonialists.

Nyamfuka

Who doesn't know the nyamfuka?[2]
I've sounded this admonition time and again.
I'll do so again: One man's meat,
Is poison to another man.

Nyamfuka,
Too much of a delicacy could be a disease.
This is common sense,
Which is not so common.

Nyamfuka,
One man's glee,
Is another man's gloom.
Think of red meat from the Nyamfuka!

Ponder the havoc red meat from Nyamfuka,
Is wrecking on your kith and kin.
Some have grown out of proportion
On account of red meat from Nyamfuka!

Others have become hippopotamuses
As a result of red meat from Nyamfuka!
Some more have metamorphosed
Into roving mountains due to red meat.

Rapacious appetite for red meat is lethal
Make no mistake about this!
Let's consume nyamfuka meat,
But do so in moderation.

---

[2] Wild animals

Kola-Nut

Kola nut—
Natural African aphrodisiac.
No sexual innuendoes implied!

Kola nut—
Source of much needed energy--
Energy to perform.

Energy to run;
Energy to walk;
Energy to talk.

Energy to work;
Energy to dance.
Energy to drink.

Kola nut—
He that brings kola,
Brings life.

Kola nut—
Benevolent companion:
Ingredient in libations.

Part and parcel of bride price;
Pacifier in times of crises.
Kola nut—Bedfellow well met!

Lion Man

I haven't a clue why
Village folks call my dad "Lion-Man".
His real name be it Joe Kunta.
Yet no one calls him by that nomenclature.
It's hard to determine if my
Dad likes or dislikes his sobriquet.

I have tried to draw a parallel
Between my dad's innate qualities
And those of a lion to no avail.
A lion is a wild beast that lives in the wild.
My dad is a personable individual,
Humane and selfless in service.

A lion is fierce;
It roars to show anger.
My dad is calm;
He stutters to show ire.
A lion's appearance strikes fear;
My dad's demeanor inspires trust.

A lion is indomitable;
My father is…
To tell the truth,
This aspect of my dad I don't know.
I have no idea why
Village folks call my dad "Lion-Man."

Rite of Passage

Wondering what this means?
Our part of the globe
Is replete with customs
Of many shapes and colors
From time immemorial.

Some good; others life-threatening.
The rite of circumcision—mutilation of
Male and female genitals is one such custom.
The rationale behind this time-honored
Tradition defies reason.

Some contend it's a rite of passage
From childhood to adulthood,
Citing the inculcation of life skills;
Others think it's a barbaric culture
Which scars initiates in body and mind.

Whether or not this contentious
Ritual ought to be discarded remains
A moot point, the more so because
It has its proponents and opponents;
Its merits and demerits.

Kontri Sunday

What's this word?
What's it worth?
For the *Ndobo* it means native Sabbath,
Memorable day to keep holy.

Kontri Sundays are welcome
Whenever they come.
It's amazing how soon we forget
About *Kontri* Sundays.

The significance of such days,
These are days to remember,
And not put on the back burner
Once the event is over.

Regardless of the time of the year,
Kontri Sundays are a time to share,
Time to celebrate,
And time to jubilate.

And while we indulge in good cheer
We should never kill the sacred dear.
The good beer we share on *Kontri* Sunday
Should be shared by all and sundry every day.

Come- no-go

A wide gamut of insidious
Ailments afflict humanity today,
The mother of them all is *Come-no-go*[3]
Disease of the mind akin to skin disease.

This canker has tentacles
Manifesting itself in a myriad forms—
Racism, xenophobia, jingoism,
Chauvinism, misogyny, misanthropy.

Humanity is locked in a deadly
Battle with purveyors of *Come no go*.
It's a lose-lose battle,
Believe or not.

---

[3] Disease of the skin that persists and resists all cures.

Radio One-Battery

There's an ingenious way
Folks south of the Sahara
Transmit news from one
Cardinal point to another—
Simply by word of mouth.

White folks call it grapevine;
Black folks brand it 'Radio One-Battery.'
People in far-flung villages
Have no access to social media—
Electronic or print media.

They simply go by word of mouth
Which travels to all the
Nooks and crannies.
My folks have dubbed it 'Bush Radio'
Others have christened it 'Radio-One-Battery.'

Mammy Wagon[4]

Leave the driving to us.
The foregoing catch-phrase,
A far cry from shrewd
Business demagoguery.

Symbol of the rectitude
That epitomizes the
Greyhound corporate ethic
In Uncle Sam.

Got a feel of it
On the occasion of my maiden
Trip to Appleton-Wisconsin via New York.
Leave the driving to us.

Male drivers like female conductors:
Personable, dutiful, immaculate
And forever time-conscious.
Leave the driving to us.

Greyhound's corporate culture--
Priceless ethos for
People-oriented enterprise,
Leave the driving to us.

---

[4] Grey Hound

Nations within the Nation

Oneida
Potawatomi,
Ojibwe,
Menominee,
Ho-chunk,
Stock-Bridge Monsee
One entity,
One lingo,
One heritage.

These are the aboriginal peoples,
Of the Americas robbed of tribal lands
By the pilgrim fathers from yonder,
When they first set foot here,
Fleeing from English religious persecution.
Remember Mayflower?
Remember dances with wolves?
Remember the Westward Expansion?
They came from afar.

Native American nations,
American Indians,
Where are they now?
Extinct or quarantined?
Confined to the reservations,
Beguiled by the fallacy of
"Nation within the nation'.
Proprietors of Casinos.

Languages banished,
Cultures eroded,

From the ashes
Of the moribund BIA[5]
Shall rise the new Indian Nation,
Like the proverbial phoenix
Intent on exacting a pound of flesh.
Time does not heal all wounds.

---

[5] Bureau of Indian Affairs. The Bureau of Indian Affairs' mission is to enhance the quality of life, to promote economic opportunity, and to carry out the responsibility to protect and improve the trust assets of American Indians, Indian tribes and Alaska Natives.

Colored People's Time

It beggars belief that at this time and age
Quite a few folks continue to cling unto the
Concept of Native Time,
Or Colored People's Time!

Oftentimes, I hide my face in shame as
I see my brethren walk leisurely into a
A board room to attend a meeting
That started many hours ago!

The concept of Native Time
Stems from a primitive mindset
That confines the colored person
To reading time by observing his shadow.

The notion of CPT
Obligates the black person to read time
By observing movements of the sun
And moon, or listening to the crow of the cock.

Native Time confines us to counting
Rivers, brooks and hillocks
In order to measure distances
Between our towns and cities.

Decency dictates that we
Be punctual at all times.
Punctuality is the hallmark of the civilized.
It is testimony of our respect for other people's time.

Son-of-the-Soil

Son-of-the-Soil.
I pour libation because
I'm a Son-of-the-Soil.

Son-of-the-Soil.
I'm circumcised because
I'm a Son-of-the-Soil.

I graduated from the
Initiation school because
I'm a Son-of-the-Soil.

I'm a full-fledge member
Of the Kwifon[6] because
I'm a Son-of-the-Soil.

Son-of-the-Soil.
I beat the Samba[7] drum because
I'm a Son-of-the-Soil.

Son-of-the-Soil.
I dance the Manjong[8] because
I'm a Son-of-the-Soil.

Son of the Soil
I pay the Lobola[9] because
I'm a son-of- the-Soil.

---

[6] Secret society
[7] Traditional dance
[8] Traditional dance
[9] Bride price

Wherever I go,
Wherever I am,
Wherever I shall be,
I remain a Son-of-the-Soil

Ongola

When the winds of change
Blew over sub-Saharan Africa in the 1990's,
Ongola[10] was not spared.
Many were convinced that
The messianic era had dawned.
Little did they know that every
Silver lining harbors a dark cloud.

And so it was that
While the populace
Wined and dined in jubilation,
Kingmakers and spin doctors
Busied themselves in
Concocting stratagems to
Perpetuate their tenure in office.

Under heavy grub and booze,
The people snoozed.
Then and only then did they
Reckon that those winds of change
Were indeed earthquakes.
Perestroika and Glasnost
Became Belletics[11] and Witch-hunting.

---

[10] Cameroon
[11] Politics of the stomach

Aborigines

The term 'aborigine' derives
From Latin meaning
'From the beginning.'
Applicable to the first people
Of any nation, it connotes
Different things to different people.

The Australoid,
The aborigines of Australia.
This nomadic group are comprised
Of tribes and clans.
That transport worldview
Sensibilities and artifacts.

The San or Bushmen,
First people of Southern Africa.
Inhabitants of the Kalahari Desert.
Cut off from mundane world,
They are branded bushmen,
In denigration of their base lifestyle.

The Sioux,
Native Americans,
Aborigines of North America
Squatting on the reservations,
They're not a nation apart;
They're a 'nation' within the nation.

The pygmies,
Original tribes of equatorial
Africa and South–East Asia.

Leading an arboreal life.
They too are aboriginal,
Earliest inhabitants of the region.

Mores

Bulala, test of manhood.
Bulala, wrestling bout.
Bulala, annual tug-of-war.
Bulala, a trial of strength
Mastermined by village monarchs
Motivated by the desire to
Betroth their unwed daughters
To valiant subjects.

Bulala, acid test of prowess.
Semi-nude youngsters
Bubbling with energy
Armed to the teeth with long
Whips made out of hide,
Combatants fight like wounded lions.
Winning the hand of the princess
Being no mean feat,
Contestants fight to kill!

Ontological Wisdom

Great Words

There are great words in our language.
 One of such words is "Thanks."

There are great words in our lingo.
Two of such words are "Forgive me."

There are great words in our patois.
Three of such words are "I love you."

Take time to express gratitude,
To give thanks is to be appreciative.

Take time to ask for forgiveness,
To err is human and to forgive is divine.

Take time to love,
Unconditional love begets happiness.

A Word to the Wise

If you're going to spend your entire life
Stewing over people who've betrayed
Your love, you'll die many times
Before your real death.
Take it easy; it's a fact of life.

If you're going to spend your whole life
Whining about people who've betrayed
Your friendship,
You'll die many times before your real death.
Take it easy; it's the only thing that ever was.

If you're going to spend your entire life
Complaining about people who've betrayed
Your confidence, you'll die several times
Before your real death.
Take it easy; it's the flip side of life.

If you're going to spend your whole life
Being bitter about people who've betrayed
Your trust, you'll die several times
Before your real death.
Take it easy; that's the irony of life.

If you're going to spend your entire life
Brooding over people who've betrayed
Your kindness, you'll die many times
Before your real death.
Take it easy; it's a natural part of life.

Vantage Point

Life may be a bed of roses to you;
To me it's a long haul.
It all depends on vantage point.

Wealth may mean materialism to you;
To me it's rich spirituality.
It all depends on vantage point.

Religion may be opium of the poor to you;
To me it's communion with God.
It all depends on vantage point.

You may find solace in substance abuse;
To me addiction is tantamount to suicide.
It all depends on vantage point.

Your modus vivendi may be
A tooth for a tooth; an eye for an eye.
To me it's give to Caesar what's Caesar's,

And to God what's God's.
See! World view is everything;
It all depends on vantage point.

Words of Wisdom

Those who've never
Walked a long rocky road,
Have no idea what an ordeal
Life's journey might be.

Those who've never
Been homeless,
Have no idea what it means
To be without a roof over one's head.

Those who've never
Known thirst,
Have no idea what it means
To not have a drop of water to drink.

Those who've never
Slept on an empty stomach,
Have no idea what famine means.
Seeing is believing.

Those who've never
known poverty,
Have no idea what indigence means.
Poverty diminishes human dignity.

Those who've never
Been severed from parental apron strings,
Have no idea what is means to
Be a self-made man.

Those who've never
Ever been barren,
Have no idea what it means to be childless.
Kids are a great gift from God.

Those who've never
Lost a parent,
Have no idea what it means to be orphaned.
Parents are a precious gift from Heaven.

Those who've never
Lost a spouse,
Have no idea what it means to be widowed.
Widowhood is a psychological burden.

Seeing the other side of life
Is always an illusion
Until you step into the shoes of others,
And then reality dawns on you!

Laissez-Faire

The essence of good parenting
In our day and time
Cannot be overemphasized.
Good kids are not born;
They are made.

The onus is on all parents
To constantly groom their
Offspring so they grow up
To be social assets; not liabilities.
The child is the man is the making.

It's not enough to give birth.
The real job of good
Parenting begins at childbirth.
And that's where most of us fall short!
Society is saddled with thorny problems!

Our schools are teeming
With juvenile delinquents
Who have become
Intractable social problem.
Who's to blame?

Our correctional homes
Are replete with juvenile offenders
Who have become an
The scourge of society
Through no fault of their own.

Our prisons are full
Of young adults who have become
Society's albatrosses
This shouldn't be so
If we all did our job well.

Savoir-Vivre

Good neighborliness is priceless,
In times of war; in times of peace.
Speak to people; make them feel welcome.
There's nothing as nice as
A cheerful word of greeting.

If you would have friends,
Be a friend yourself.
Speak and act as if everything
You do is a genuine pleasure.
Cultivate savoir-faire.

Be genuinely interested in people.
Call people by their names.
The sweetest music to anyone's ear
Is the sound of their own name.
Forge a modus vivendi.

Smile at people.
It takes seventy-eight muscles
To frown and only fourteen to smile.
Be generous with praise;
And cautious with criticism.

Backbone

We need to recognize
The importance of the family
As the backbone of every successful society.
A society that undermines the family
Is a society doomed to fail.

Divorce is a canker
Tearing apart the very
Fabric of contemporary society.
Greed is the culprit.
That shouldn't be the case!

Sham marriages are a travesty.
Illegal cohabitations,
Are pseudo-marriages.
They make a mockery of matrimony.
That shouldn't be the case!

Single parenthood is the
End product of wedlock
Built on sandy soil.
That shouldn't be the case!
Take time to know your partner.

It is high time we called off the bluff.
It's time to lay a solid
Foundation for generations to come.
Willy-nilly we are answerable to posterity.
The family is the backbone of society.

Life's an Attitude

This is a fact of life.
One of the greatest pleasures
Of living is that no one would
Help another without ultimately
Helping themselves.

In this fast-paced world of ours,
It's easy to get so engrossed
In oneself that one forgets to
Lend a helping hand when need be.
Life's an attitude.

The essence of life is not
To stand for everything there is.
Rather, it's to stand for something
That makes a difference in the
Community of humans.

Willy-nilly,
We're in this ontological
Tug-of-war together.
By this token, it makes sense to contribute
To the common good by all means necessary.

Termites

Termites don't build;
They destroy.
The folks at the helm of
Affairs are termites!

They've destroyed the national economy.
They've destroyed the education system.
They've destroyed our moral fiber.
They've destroyed the morale of workers.

The folks at the helm of
In Ongola[12] are termites!
They've destroyed our self-confidence.
They've destroyed our self-worth.

They're hard at work destroying
The legacy of our founding fathers.
Termites are in charge of our collective destiny.
Shall they make or mar? It's time for fumigation!

---

[12] Cameroon

Free Ride

Life's not a roller coaster.
There are tons of folks out there
With the strong conviction that
Life's an amusement ride.
That's living in fool's paradise!
He that desires victory prepares to win.

Life's not a roller coaster.
There are zillions of individuals
Out there who believe
That the world owes them a debt.
What debt? May I ask?
The world owes you nothing!

If you fail to plan
You plan to fail.
This is natural law.
You reap what you sow.
Life's not a roller coaster.
Bitter Pill indeed!

There are lots of people
Out there who think that
Their survival is contingent
Upon the good will of others.
That's a fallacy!
Life is survival of the fittest.

Poverty of Affluence

What's this word?
Have you ever pondered
What poverty may mean
To different people in
Different circumstances?

Poverty is pregnant with meaning.
To be poor is to lack
The basic necessities of life.
But a childless couple
Living in opulence is doubly poor.

How many times
Have you heard a rich man
Lament that he'd give everything
He owns in exchange for a child?
That too is poverty in affluence!

To be poor is to lack intellectual baggage.
How many times have
You heard an unlettered rich person
Say that he'd give away everything
He has just to be able to read and write?

To be irreligious is to be poor in spirit.
How many times
Have you heard the agnostic
Express the desire to know God?
Lack of faith is abject poverty.

The next time
You think of the lexeme 'poverty',
Consider its many facets.
Poverty has many faces—
Visible and invisible.

Quiet Peacemakers

I have half a mind to
Turn and live with sheep.
They are forever tranquil.
I watch them in utter admiration,
Envious of their calm disposition.

They do not whine and fret
About what tomorrow
Has in store for them.
They don't anger me with tales
Of money-laundering.

None amasses wealth.
No one builds castles in the air.
None abuses power.
No one kills its own kind.
None indulges in debauchery.

Not a single one harbors lurid desires.
They all accept their lot in life.
I have half a mind to
Turn and live with sheep.
They have risen above petty jealousies.

Footprints of Destiny

Man is an unwilling pawn
On the chessboard of gods.
Regardless of one's ambitions,
No matter our aspirations,
Destiny always catches up with us.

In this guise, it makes sense
To make haste slowly.
Seek fair play in all you do,
Shun foul play in everything you do.
The end does not always justify the means.

Before warned is before armed.
What goes around comes around.
On doomsday we shall be answerable
For our deeds, each man by himself.
Before the Almighty. No escape route!

Clando Driver's Wisdom

Straddled between the
North and the South
As we are, puts all and sundry
Astride two antithetical worlds—
Local versus global mores—
Indigenous to the Atlantic and the Sahara.

Under the circumstance,
Our hybrid nature is
But a fait accompli.
Reason why it behooves
Us all to embrace the best
Of both worlds at all costs.
That's clando[13] driver's wisdom.

---

[13] Clandestine taxi driver

White Ants

Might is not size.
The white ant is
Pretty minuscule,
Yet in less than no time
It will demolish a baobab.

Little nations
Like big nations make
Up this planetary concave.
Each one has a vital role to play
In this community of nations.

On the chessboard
Of nations there's no room
for foul play; do unto others
What you would
Have them do unto you.

No nation has
Monopoly over war-mongering.
The pacifists of today may
Become the belligerents of tomorrow.
The Hawks of today may become doves tomorrow.

We're all liable to vulnerability.
It has happened elsewhere;
It can happen here.
He that has been bitten by a snake
Flees when he sees a millipede.

Fate of a Continent

It beats logic
To believe that we will
Save this continent by
Balkanizing it into tribal enclaves.
This kind of social
Engineering spells doom.

The future of Africa
Resides in its collective vision.
We must unite behind
A common goal to address
Developmental challenges.
African intelligentsia must

Pick up the cudgels and do battle
With foes of Africa regardless of provenance.
They must bear the flickering torch
That leads us out of darkness.
This is not a task for outsiders.
Africans must unite!

Time is Money

Time is pregnant with aphorisms—
Time and tide wait for no one,
A stitch in time saves nine,
Procrastination is the thief of time.
There's time for everything:
Time to work and time to rest.

In bread-and-butter world,
Time is money--
Modus vivendi for money sharks,
Humanity and time are locked
In a vicious race headed for nowhere.
Time is fleeting in mundane world.

Folks can't sleep anymore!
Folks can't eat anymore!
Folks can't rest anymore!
Folks can't play anymore!
Folks can't commune anymore!
Life has become one big emergency!

Homes are ripped asunder--
Parents vie with one another
For control of time
Children left to their own devices
Have the leeway to do to their heart's content.
I wonder when this infernal
Rat-race will ever come to an end.

Cultural Relativism

What's this culture?
What does it mean?
Culture is a hydra
With many tentacles.

Culture is the planting
Of crops for human consumption.
Hard to fathom what the world would be
Without agriculture.

Culture is also the customs,
Civilization and achievements
Of a particular people at a given time.
Hard to imagine what the peoples of the globe
Would be without cultural identities.

Culture is furthermore the norms,
Attitudes, values and belief systems
Deeply ingrained in the psyche of an institution.
Hard to think of a school without a culture—
The complex pattern of behaviors that typify each school.

Corporate culture is
The rules and regulations
That govern the way folks do business.
Every enterprise has
A corporate culture sufficient unto itself.

The underworld has a culture.
There is honor among thieves.
Hard to think of the narcotic trade without a culture.

The principles and behaviors
That rule the drug market is the drug culture.

So my friend, next time
You ponder the term 'culture',
Remember that it's a hybrid term
And therefrom stems the concept
Of Cultural relativism.

Musings

Myth of Sisyphus

Man and fate are on a collision course.
Man's race against destiny
Is like the race of Sisyphus
Against a recalcitrant rolling stone.
That of which Albert Camus spoke.

The cunning king of Corinth'
Punished in Hades to roll
Up a hill a huge stone which
Always rolled down again as soon
As he had brought it to the summit.

Most of us are like Sisyphus.
Celebrated Albert Camus
Captured the puzzle of Man's futile
Race against destiny
In *Le Mythe de Sisyphe*.

Disciplined Mind

Disciplined minds seek the common good,
Avoiding the company of those who holler,
For they are pernicious to the spirit.
Speak truth fearlessly
Without rancor or favor.

Steer clear of myopic competitors.
If you compare yourself with others,
You will be grumpy and bitter.
For always there will be greater
Persons than yourself.

Without rancor,
Vengeance or spleen,
Seek fair play at all times.
For injustice done unto one,
Is injustice done unto many.

Walks of Life

I can't help but liken life to the first
Steps of a baby learning to walk.
You may be a guru in one walk of life.
In yet another you are a neophyte.

Numbed by pangs of self-inflation,
Many of us trudge through
Life reeling in excruciating pain,
Oblivious of the fact that
It is okay to seek help.

No man is an island
Sufficient unto himself.
We are in this together.
The travails of existence are daunting.
We had better brave them in tandem.

Coconut

The coconut is Earth's toughest seed.
Well equipped to survive
The vagaries of life's journey,
This seed is able to accomplish
An aquatic journey of circa
Ten thousand miles against all odds!

How many of God's creatures
Are like the coconut?
How soon do we falter and
Succumb to the vicissitudes of life?
The coconut owes it resilience
To its protective outer cover.

If I may ask, are you a coconut?
Do you have a protective shield?
My shield is the Lord Jesus:
My Shepherd and Redeemer.
That's why I am like a coconut.
 The coconut, hard nut to crack!

Chains

I once was a dipsomaniac
But Jesus broke the chains
And set me free.

I once was a nymphomaniac
But Jesus broke the chains
And set me free.

I once was a porn addict
But Jesus broke the chains
And set me free.

I once found solace in substance abuse
But Jesus broke the chains
And set me free.

I once had the temper of a wasp
But Jesus broke the chains
And set me free.

I once was agnostic
But Jesus broke the chains
And set me free.

Jesus Christ is the same
Yesterday, today and forever.
He did it for me; He will do it for you.

Nemesis

Evildoers perceive themselves
As parallel lines that never meet.
Nothing could be more fallacious.
Mountains and hills don't move
Yet humans are mobile animals.

The evil that we do
Haunts us ad infinitum.
That which you harvest
Is that which you planted.
That's the law of cause and effect.

When one sows the wind
One reaps the whirlwind.
We're our own worst enemies
When nemesis catches up with us,
Make no mistake.

Third Eye

Watch yourself go by day in day out.
Perceive yourself as "He", not "I".
Find fault with yourself as you'd with others.
Confront yourself unabashedly.
Watch yourself go by each day.

Read meaning into your every intention,
Just like you would judge others.
Let unmitigated criticism surge through you.
Reproach yourself for every flaw.
Watch yourself go by every day.

Without taking the log out of your eyes,
Try to see the speck in the eyes of others.
Stand by and watch yourself with the third eye.
If you'd do this, it would dawn on you
That you lack the moral high ground

On which to stand and judge others.
Your love for others will grow like
Mushrooms on a decaying tree.
Stand by and watch yourself with the third eye,
If you'd do this, you'd enjoy spiritual healing.

Opium

What is this word?
What does it mean?
Religion may be
Opium for the poor.
What do you think
Is the opium for the opulent?
And the not-so-rich?
Have you ever given
Second thought to this puzzle?

As I see it,
The world is replete with
Opium of different
Shades and colors.
Ponder coital opium.
Behind every sex scandal
There lurks libido.
That too is opium.
Think of megalomania.

Power mongering is opium
For the megalomaniac.
Money is opium
For many a shark.
Behind every raw deal
There's a money-monger.
And so on, ad infinitum.
Fella, next time you talk opium,
Reckon it's got multiple faces.

Eau-de-vie

H2O, water of life.
Compound of oxygen and hydrogen.
Colorless, odorless, and tasteless.
Water touches every facet of our lives.
Water is enemy to no one.

We drink water,
We cook with water,
We bathe in water,
We swim in water,
We cultivate in water.

Over sixty percent of the human body
Is composed of water.
What would happen if the waters
Of the earth suddenly dried up?
Terrestrial life would come to a standstill!

H2O, water of life.
A flowing gift.
Lifeblood of the kingdom of
Plants, animals and humans.
Sustenance of living things.

Backwoods Mentality

To the best of my knowledge,
The swine is the lone
Beast in the animal kingdom
That devours its young when
Subjected to the pangs of hunger.

Surprisingly enough,
The human race now
Vies with pigs in the race
Toward cannibalism!
Man has become man's predator!

What with homicide,
Voluntary termination of pregnancy,
Voodoo cults, infanticide,
Witchcraft, fratricide,
You name the rest!

There's no gainsaying the fact—
The human race excels in cruelty.
Man is the architect of his own very undoing.
Little wonder the list of genocidal wars
Is as long as the Mississippi River.

Bomb Scare

Bomb scare
Hoax or reality?
Handiwork of the
Insane or psychopath?

Come to think of it
What's the rationale behind
A scare by the bomb?
Million dollar question!

Bomb scare hither and thither,
Outward manifestation of some
Manic depression or outburst
Of pent-up emotions?

Regardless of the motive behind bomb scares,
Truth be told: it scares the shit out of me!
It has dire consequences—hysteria,
Lost man-hours, wasted income...

Sins of Omission

In our folklore,
The mouth that tells
The truth does not lie.
These are words of wisdom
From golden-agers.

They quip—
When you point an accusing
Forefinger at someone,
Four are pointing at you –
Ponder that and let it sink!

When you criticize someone,
You define them not.
You define yourself—
The kind of person you are.
Sins of omission and commission cohabitate.

Wages of Sin

The wages of sin is death,
Quips a verse in the book of life.
The Holy Scriptures speak of the
Calamity that befell the cities of
Sodom and Gomorrah in days of old.
This is the fate of man when
He outlives his usefulness.

History repeats itself.
Genesis paints a dismal picture
Of man at the lowest ebb of morality—
Our era ain't any better—
Fornication, treachery, unmarried couples,
Drug addiction, sexual promiscuity,
Homicide, wife battery, adultery.

Contemporary society
Has gone a step further.
Amorality is its stock-in-trade—
Substance abuse, pornography, cyber- sex,
Teen coitus, pedophilia, dypsomania,
Kleptomania and nymphomania
And a host of others.

Modus Operandi

Recipe

To you my child,
I leave these golden
Rules for successful living:
Be nice to people,
Known and unknown.
Be kind to brothers and sisters.
Be fair to others,
Keep yourself busy.
An idle mind is the devil's workshop!

Never tell a lie to anyone;
Never gossip about people;
Never talk ill of others;
The penalty for sin is death!
Never spend money mindlessly.
Never take that which does not belong to you.
Never borrow things from others.
Never borrow money.
Strive always to be self-sufficient.

Go to church every Sunday;
Read your Bible constantly;
Fear of the Lord is the beginning of wisdom;
Avoid blind imitation;
Listen to advice!
Follow these precepts
Day and night without relent.
These words, my son, are my
Legacy to you and yours.

Ghost Town Operation

Breaking a bad law is a patriotic act.
So it was during the famous
Opération villes mortes[14]
That almost ran Mr. Paul Biya
Out of his hideout in Mvog-Meka
This globe is replete with anti-people laws.
Should the populace comply with such laws?
There comes a time in the life of a people
When unpopular laws have to be flouted.

Where would the Germany of Adolf Hitler be today
Had it not dawned on the people that it was time
To toss Nazi laws into the trashcan of history?
Where would Gaullist France be today
Had it not occurred to the people
To jettison monarchical edicts into the
Garbage can of history during the French Revolution?
There comes a time in the life of a people
When unpopular laws have to be transgressed.

Where would Verwoerdian South Africa be today
Had the downtrodden not deemed it time
To throw apartheid laws into the dustbin of history?
Where would Uncle Sam be today
Had Americans not said enough is enough
to Jim Crow laws? Didn't Rosa Parks say:
"I am tired" (of unwholesome laws?)
There comes a time in the life of a people
When unpopular laws have to be trampled upon.

---

[14] Ghost Town Operation

The legality of a law doesn't make it fair.
Its humaneness does make it binding.
Civil disobedience is no bane; it's a boon.
 In the wake of the Presidential Fiasco in 1992,
My people said, *trop c'est trop*[15]
And spat on Biya's sham laws.
There comes a time in the life of a people
When unpopular laws have to be trampled upon.
That's what transpired during Ghost Town Operation.

---

[15] Enough is enough

Barrel of the Gun

He that seeks peace,
Prepares for war.
An armed nation,
Is a safe nation.
These are admonitions
To take with a grain of salt.
Those who declare,
War do not know that
War consumes its perpetrators.

The mayhem wrecked
By gun-toting youngsters
In and around school precincts
Bears crystal testimony to
The folly that fuels
The craze for firearms.
NRI, Culprit Number One.
Paranoia, Culprit Number Two
Ego, Culprit Number Three.

Places of learning
Have become war zones haunted
By trigger-crazy delinquents.
In every nook and cranny,
The specter of death
Hangs over our heads
Like the sword of Damocles.[16]
Who's the next cadaver?
Who is the next fodder for cannon?

---

[16] The Sword of Damocles-is an allusion to the imminent and ever-present peril faced by those in positions of power.

The media has further
Emboldened a great many folks
By churning out the hollow
Propaganda that a gun-free
Nation is an unsafe nation.
That's hogwash!
That's old wives' tale!
That's a tall tale!
Call off the bluff!

Pandemonium

A jilted boyfriend storms into
A girlfriend's apartment,
Clobbers her to death!
There's pandemonium.

An armed cuckolded husband
Charges into a love nest,
Clobbers spouse and philanderer!
There's pandemonium.

A high school student flunks her finals,
Takes entire faculty hostage,
Fires fatal shots at professors who drop dead!
There's pandemonium.

I can't make
Head or tail of this
Pandemonium.
Can you?

Clansman's Dynamics

Branding the Neenah Foundry Co.
A mere factory is to miss the point.
As I see it this place is a beehive—
Some are manipulating the
Clansman dynamics (robotics);
Others welding pieces together.

Some trimming castings;
Many more driving fork-lifts
At break-neck speed.
A few more programming in quasi-hysteria,
In this hub of human activities time is money;
Making money as fast as possible.

Circa one thousand heavily
Tattooed men and women
Work real hard for the money.
Every one's task is well cut out.
Neenah Foundry in Wisconsin,
Epitome of Capitalism.

Other Vistas

Roots

A long time ago,
The winds of corporate greed
Blew *Toubabs* from yonder
To the shores of the Congo River[17]
In quest of human cargo.

That was the genesis
Of the cruelest act of man's
Inhumanity to fellow human beings.
They purchased 'cargo' from the
Hands of benighted natives.

They shipped them under the
Most humiliating conditions
To southern plantations.
The transit was an ordeal.
Thousands gave up the ghost.

The hardship was too hard to bear.
Thousands more were jettisoned
Into crocodile-infested waters
For attempting to regain freedom.
The was the Trade.

Massa and nigger was the lingo
That differentiated the enslaved from the master.
Yet the Massa was no master of his libido!
He had coitus with my shackled sisters,
And fathered many mulattoo.

---

[17] The Congo River, formerly the Zaire River is Africa's most powerful river and the second most voluminous river in the world.

The Massa re-christened my siblings niggers.
Kunta Kinte was reborn as Toby.
That was the fate of them all.
This act was no fad on
The part of the Toubab.

Take away a man's cultural identity,
You make a nonentity out of him!
The truth is bitter but must be spoken:
A good Toubab
Is a dead Toubab.

No Man's Land

This land is no man's land!
It is land of immigrants.
This land belongs to no one.
It belongs to everyone--
You, me, he, she, they.

All and sundry have moved
Here from other climes.
Isn't it an irony of sorts,
Though, that some inhabitants of this land
Are relegated to second status on account of bias?

Bigotry governs this land!
Ignorance is a canker eating deep
Into the fabric of this land.
Greed is the green-eyed
Monster on this land.

Those who arrogate
To themselves the label
'Autochthons' know little about
The history of this land.
Ignorance is not bliss.

Guantanamo

Guantanamo--
Naval base prison à Cuba;
Nemesis of the Djimtete[18]
How can we be judge and
Defendant at the same time?

Guantanamo à Cuba—
Held on perpetual lease
From Cuba who has no
Control whatsoever over the
Notorious prison.

Guantanamo à Cuba—
Home to 650-odd prisoners
From all walks of life,
All deprived of inalienable rights!
Captives held in this dungeon.

Inmates have no access whatsoever
To any form of legal counsel.
Requiem for Habeas Corpus!
Guantanamo à Cuba
Our dirty linen washed in public.

Guantanamo à Cuba—
Judicial aberration!
Symbol of legal limbo,
Into which no law-abiding nation
Should ever wittingly stray.

---

[18] Big shot

Amerika

America is best described
By one epithet—freedom.
Amerika is more than a mere
Geographical expression.
It is the land of the free and the brave.
Home to institutionalized equality.

Amerika is a dream—
The American dream—
Home, job and family.
A dream nursed by dignity and strength
Of common human nature.
This is what Amerika is all about—

A land wherein all races, creeds
Ethnicities thrive in ONE meeting pot.
That's the uniqueness of Amerika—
Land where the son of a former slave and
That of the erstwhile slave master
May dream the same dreams.

Bygone Times

Remembrance of bygone times,
Life's replete with points in
Time when we are faced
With the ominous task
Of making momentous decisions.

My relocation to Uncle Sam
Was one such moment.
Bag and baggage,
Adieu to age-old chums,
No turning back.

Lured by unaccomplished dreams,
Desire to start life from scratch,
Not an easy decision to make,
Regardless of all hopes and promises
That posterity may hold in store.

After vacillating
For days on end I resolved to
Take the bait.
March 21, 2001 was
That momentous day.

Hillbrow

Humanity is replete
With examples of cities that have
Degenerated from luxuriance to decrepitude.
Hillbrow in Johannesburg—City of Gold
is a patent case in point.

                        In days of apartheid,
Hillbrow was the heartbeat
                        of Azanian Economy.
In this day and age, though,
                        the city enjoys the pride
of place as the crime capital
                        of the world.

                  Men of the underworld call the shots.
Drug lords duck and dive
                        as they peddle marijuana and
hard drugs
                        left, right and center,
                        in   full   glare   of   law
enforcement officers.

                        Armed   robbers   mug   and
strangulate
                        victims with impunity.
                        Conmen   from   all   the   nooks
and crannies
                        Of   the   globe   rip   off
unsuspecting strangers
                        At gunpoint in broad daylight.

Child whores vie ferociously
With haggard old-timers for scarce clientele.

These and countless other crimes have

Earned Jo'burg the epithet 'Megatomb'.

Hillbrow has become a euphemism for hellhole.

Nouvelle France

Perambulating in Quebec City
Is like turning the pages of
A book replete with pictures
Reminiscent of the past.
The view changes on
Every street corner.

Quebec lingo for "where the river narrows."
Samuel de Champlain native of Brouage in France,
Founder of this historic city in 1608
On the north shore of the majestic
St Lawrence River that harbors history.
Nouvelle France – a world of its own.

Quebec City home to
Denizens and aboriginal peoples—
Abenakis, Algonquins, Atikamekw,
Malecites, Micmacs, Inuit, Naskapis,
Hurons, Wendat, Iroquois and more.
Quebec, nation within the Nation.

Contemporary Quebec City,
The Jewel of World Heritage
In UNESCO nomenclature;
Numerous wonders do it justice—
Notre Dame Bascilica, Château Frontenac,
Place d'Armes, Quartier Latin, Montmorency…

Côte de la Montagne, Mural of Quebecers,
Escaliers Casse-Cou, Place Royale, the Citadel,
Basilique Sainte Anne de Beaupré, Musée des

Augustins, Musée de la civilisation,
Quartier Petit Champlain and la Cabane à sucre.
These are the secrets of Quebec City.

Quebec reposes in its multifaceted characters.
With every step you take the view changes—
A new panorama unfolds
Before your very own eyes
New France a veritable
North American Treasure.
Quebec City,
Marvelous delight,
The city's motto
Je me souviens—
I remember,
Speaks volumes.

The Human Condition

Alter Ego

I'm at war with myself
I've been told to be like the other;
Act like the other;
Talk like the other;
Work hard at impersonation.

Why must I be like the other?
Rid myself of myself. Why?
I know that the value of
A diamond derives from
The uniqueness of each gem!

Why then would I auction my personhood?
Dress like them. Why?
Eat like them. Why
Talk like them. Why?
Even smell like them. Why?

Why would I embrace the Other?
Worship their gods?
Disown my gods? Why?
I know that by seeking to be the other
I become a counterfeit!

Manacles

Man is born free
But entangled in chains everywhere—
Fetters of daily toil;
Chains of substance abuse.

Man is born free
But lives in shackles of moral crisis;
Chains of decadence;
Manacles of infidelity.

Man is born free
But lives in chains of ineptitude;
Bonds of fundamentalist bigotry;
Chains of imperialist yoke.

Man lives in bondage
Self-imposed servitude,
Enchained in parochialism!
Mental debility.

Mankind is hard at
Work decimating womenfolk.
Womankind is engrossed in the
Task of undoing mankind!

Each passing day portends
Woe for humanity,
Man's calamitous descent into the
Dungeon of nothingness is unstoppable.

Dog Days

In bygone days,
It was heartening to see
Grandparents and grandchildren
Cohabite under one roof.
Not anymore!

The god of capitalism and
Individualism has decreed that
We put our senior citizens in quarantine.
Left to their own devices in
Assisted living homes and hospices.

In bygone days,
These hapless golden-agers
Didn't languish in utter desolation.
They're part and parcel of the household,
Not anymore!

Glued to wheelchairs;
Others bedridden;
Many more ravaged by senile
Dementia and Alzheimer's disease.
We must keep them at arm's length.

They bid time,
Awaiting the last moment.
We've thrown our sense of
Duty to the dogs! Shame on us!
Dog Days aren't over[19].

---

[19] Dog Days Are Over" is a song by English indie rock band Florence and the Machine from their debut album *Lungs* (2009).

Bulimia Nervosa

I have a madding craving for food;
I long for junk food,
I eat like a horse—
At home, at work, in my car, everywhere.
Alas, this bulimia's taking me to Hades.
It's a bane not than a boon.
My physique speaks volumes—

I am a roving mountain;
I have grown a second stomach
The infamous spare tire,
My cheeks sag,
My legs heavy as lead.
I suffer from insatiable hunger,
Yet I throw up in the wake of each meal!

I gasp for breath.
I am ill at ease!
I am on the horns of a dilemma—
I abhor obesity
And yet I dread anorexia,
Bulimia Nervosa,
Not a friend well met!

Persona Non Grata

It all began like a trickle.
As days fled by,
Tiny little drops grew into a flood:
Your teaching leaves much to be desired!
We're worried about your pedagogy!
You seem to have bitten
Off more than you can chew!

Your first commitment
Is Roosevelt Middle School.
The admonitions flew like a cascade.
Hardly did I know
That in these precincts
Wolves dress up in sheep's skin
I smelt a rat.

Amidst phony grins
Machiavelli was hard
At work concocting my ouster.
On that gloomy fateful day;
The bombshell fell:
On Monday you'll be reassigned to
The IT Department of the district.

Your teaching contract
Will also not be renewed!
It's hard to tell who erred in all this.
One thing for sure:
The omnipotent is the arbiter.
The evil that men do lives with them.
Nemesis is an indomitable hunter.

Ere long, he'll catch up
With predators YONDER.
There'll be loud mourning
And gnashing of teeth.
In the abode of peddlers
Of half-truths and shenanigans.
Make no mistake!

Kid Power

As far as parental duty goes,
I believe some of us
Have misplaced priorities.
'Children First'!
What's this phrase?
What does it mean?

Should kids call the shoots
At the expense of parents?
Does it mean rights
Without responsibilities?
Rights without duties!
Did I hear that?

The word 'freedom' is
A word most abused by kids.
Freedom ought not to carry
The germ of recklessness.
Kid power a lethal weapon
To be handled with caution.

Cup-a-Tea

You abhor my accoutrement
That's your cup-a-tea.
I gotta wear what I wanna wear.
No freaking business of yours!

You detest my mannerisms
That's your cup-a-tea.
I gotta do what I wanna do.
Damn it!

You hate my lingo
That's your cup-a-tea.
I gotta speak what I wanna speak.
Couldn't care less whose horse is gored.

You dislike my demeanor
That's your cup-a-tea.
I gotta be what I wanna be.
Mind your f...cking business!

You don't like my workaholic lifestyle
That's your cup-a-tea.
I gotta do what I wanna do.
Bask in your mediocre paradise !

You disdain my effrontery
That's your cup-a-tea.
I gotta say what I wanna say.
Son of a bitch!

You scorn my teetotaler mode of living
That's your cup-a-tea.
I gotta do what it takes to stay sober.
Got nothing to do with Bacchus!

You loathe my worldview
That's your cup-a-tea.
I gotta see the world through my own prism,
I"ve got no tolerance for myopia!

You desecrate my creed
That's your cup-a-tea.
I gotta worship what I wanna worship.
Everyone's got their own fetish.

You denigrate my mores
That's your cup-of-tea.
I belong where I am.
Everyone's got their own traditions.

You despise my color
That's your cup-a-tea.
I am who I am now and forever.
Everyone's got their own pigmentation.

To everyone their own kind
I am who I am ad infinitum.
I don't wanna be y'all
Hope I'm crystal clear.

Tabula Rasa

It's a new year!
If yesterday was
Marked by impropriety,
Wouldn't it better matter to
Turn over a new leaf today?

It's a new year!
If the past was devoid of goals,
Wouldn't it be worthwhile to
Set attainable goals now?
New times new precepts.

It's a new year!
If bygone times were bedeviled
By billingsgate and debauchery,
Wouldn't it be proper to
Clean the slate and start anew?

It's a new year!
If yesteryears were
Times of slothful lethargy,
Wouldn't it be a good thing to
Turn things around?

If the days gone by
Were squandered on
Whining and scheming,
Wouldn't it pay off to
Make a U-turn for the better?

If the previous year
Was whiled away
On backstabbing,
Bickering and gossip,
Wouldn't it be rewarding to quit now?

If you wore the cap of
Egotistic bigotry in the past
Don't you think it's high
Time you donned the hat of altruism?
It's a New Year.

My yesterdays were dogged
By pessimistic self-doubt
Today I doff the hat of
Compulsive optimism
Because it's a New Year.

Summum Bonum

Brouhaha

So much chattering about nothing!
Equality in educational opportunities
In these precincts;
But come to think of it,
It's a caste system where the rich get the best.

Sore point is:
Funding for schooling stems
From state and local governments,
Notably from local taxes
Within the school district.

Implication?
The rich are blessed
With top-notch schools.
Conversely, the poor make do with a pittance,
Such is the paradox of apartheid-styled education!

Camp Fire

What's this word?
What's it worth?
Camp fires are welcome
Whenever they come.

Camp fires are distractions
From our daily attractions.
While we bask in actions,
In the warmth of a campfire.

We should never misfire
By shooting at the live deer
That lies in good cheer,
Near a camp fire.

The good cheer
Ushered by a camp fire each day
Should be shared by folks every day,
With lots of beer.

Checks-for-Degrees

This world of ours
Is replete with myriad vendors.
But the mother of them all
Is the gray matter merchant.

The nomenclature is legion—
Instructors, teachers, professors,
Evangelists, pastors, priests,
You name them.

All embarked on the ignoble task of
Destroying green minds.
Whether we are teachers or parents,
Our primary duty is to facilitate learning.

We are lifelong learners
Strong in the belief
That he who has learned
Nothing has nothing to teach.

The nature of our society dictates
That we learn or perish.
Not an old wife's tale!
Knowledge is power.

The ability to learn from the cradle
To the grave sets us apart from beasts.
How come we've given leeway to
Shenanigans in academia?

Hawks

Just or unjust war?
That is the question!
The specter of our men and women
In uniform armed with weapons of mass
Deception acting unilaterally to invade other lands,
Purportedly to civilize the uncouth
Deeply violates the notion of fairness.

The chief threat to
Global peace in this day and time
Seems to be US not THEM.
The logic of preemptive war
Is untenable in international diplomacy.
A nation that does not respect life
Harbors the germ of its own very destruction.

An attack on one nation
Is an attack on all nations,
The comportment of our military
Has opened Pandora's Box,
Threatening to let loose dogs of war,
Demons of death and destruction,
That will be our Armageddon.

A great many folks see
What I see but won't voice it.
I call a spade a spade.
An illustrious son of the universe once quipped:
The world will not be destroyed
By those who do evil but by those who

See evil and do nothing.[20]

---

[20] Quote from Albert Einstein

Baptism with Fire

Anchor Food Products, Inc.[21]
555 Hickory Farm Lane,
Legacy of Robert and Joan Follet;
Unfathomable beehive of activity!

Some are capping;
Others are inspecting.
Some are stacking,
Others are sending.

Some are packing;
Others are packaging.
Some are mixing;
Others are forklifting.

Some are cleaning;
Others are sanitizing.
So variegated are specialties
In this appetizer business.

And many are the nations represented:
Hmong, Mexican, Africans,
Polish, Indian, Chinese,
African-Americans and more.

Anchor Food Products, Inc.
A world in its own right!
Fathom what the food service would
Be without Anchor's quality products?

---

[21] Food processing company in Appleton-Wisconsin

Anathema

Racial prejudice
A is a skunk!
I call you Nigger!
In mock attempt
At denigration.
In point of fact,
I deride myself.
God the Creator
Is color blind.

I call you Nigger!
Blinded by deep-rooted
Bigotry that compartmentalizes
The universe into
Pockets of pigments.
What crippling idiocy!
In point of fact,
I live in fool's Paradise where
 Wisdom is anathema.

I call you Nigger!
My world is built
On individualism--
A self-seeking world
Where stereotyping is
An indelible hallmark.
Pity not yourself.
Pity me for I know
Not what's going on in the world.

Paradox

We're champions of democracy
Even if our polls are
Not always transparent.

We're champions of human rights
Even if we slyly perpetrate civil strife
In alien lands to our pecuniary advantage.

We're advocates of equality, justice and liberty
Even if we perceive the world
Through racial and socio-economic prisms.

We're holier than thou
Even if we bathe in
Sanctimonious hypocrisy.

We're global pace-setters
Even if our claim to
Pre-eminence is self-styled.

We think, therefore we are.
Our society, barring its
Flaws is yet the global first.

In Memoriam

Have you forgotten 9/11?
I'll never forget 9/11!
The horrific terrorist assault on the
Twin towers of the World Trade Center
And the Pentagon on September 11, 2001
Has hardened Uncle Sam's steel of resilience.

Tuesday's catastrophic collapse
Of the two towers, one after the other
And a sequence of panic in the streets
Serves as potent reminder to all and sundry
That there's villainy in our world.
Clarion call for perpetual vigilance.

America remains unfazed by the enemy's wrath.
Terrorists may shatter the steel of
Her monuments; they will not dent
The steel of her patriotism.
We stand together as one nation,
Indivisible under one God.

The Creed

To save the environment,
To restore a sense of balance
To God's creation,
Humanity needs to halt
The sin of green rape.

Thou shall hold nature in awe;
Thou shall not be the ruler of the earth;
Thou shall not be the irrational user,
Thou shall not conquer nature
For the sole purpose of enjoying life.

Let this not be misconstrued
As an endorsement of savage primitivism,
Or blatantly anti-humanism.
Harken, the earth is in the balance.
The onus is on us to safeguard the balance sacred.

Bitter Pills

Fences

Jim Crow is dead
Long live Jim Crow!
Old habits die hard.
Requiem for Jim Crow
Was sung ages ago.
Yet Jim Crow lives!

How many times
Have you been labeled nitwit
Because of the color of our skin?
How too often have we been subjected
To less than dignified treatment
On account of the texture of our hair?

How often have they branded
Us less than human in veiled terms—
The slights and cold stares?
How many times has the race card
Been used to shy away from giving merit
Where merit is due?

How often have we been
Trailed in shops for fear
That the kleptomaniacs
That we are will steal something.
That's not racial profiling, you know!
It's called the vigilante.

Come to think of it,
Ku Klux Klan (KKK)—
The hate-mongers and supremacists

Aren't dead and buried.
They've merely built
Fences around themselves.

Mass Deception

Their insatiable thirst for war
Hangs on thinly veiled falsehoods—
The liberation of oppressed peoples
Is an act of magnanimity.

The fact of the matter is their warmongering
Has nothing to do with humanitarianism—
It's all about self-aggrandizement
And quest for liquid wealth.

Empire builders are a threat to global peace.
In fact, they are our worst enemies—
The real threat to world peace is their manic
Desire to erect a grand empire.

They're in league with global terrorists.
They amass weapons of
Mass deception to our detriment.
They have the world's biggest arsenal of lethal ammo.

Faces behind Masks

There's no gainsaying the point.
This world of ours is a stage
Where every thingamabob[22] comes to act.
Garbed in multifaceted masks,
Folks make believe in all walks of life!

Foes act like friends;
Friends mistaken for foes.
Mortals play God;
Humans pass for super-humans.
Miscreants ape the pious.

This world of ours is a stage
Where self-seekers masquerade as
Selfless philanthropists. Worse still—
Servants of Satan spot the mask
Of men of God! Pedophiles!

Truth is this globe is replete with impostors.
How long shall we dress in borrowed robes?
How long shall we pull wool over the eyes of folks?
How long shall we wear masks?
I call a spade a spade; couldn't care less!

---

[22] Used to refer to or address a person or thing whose name one has forgotten, does not know, or does not wish to mention.

Fads

Life's a fad
Think of racism:
Compulsive hatred
Of other races.

Life's a fad
Think of fanaticism:
Compulsive enthusiasm
For one's idol.

Life's a fad
Think of fascism:
Compulsive authoritarian views.
That too is a fad.

Life's a fad
Ponder nihilism:
Compulsive rejection of
Religious and moral principles.

Life's a fad
Think of jingoism:
Compulsive bellicosity.
That certainly is a fad.

Life's a fad
What d'you say about chauvinism?
Compulsive prejudice
Against the fair sex.

Life's a fad

What's your thought on pedophilia?
Compulsive sexual obsession
Directed toward kids.

Life' a fad
Think of dipsomania:
Compulsive craving for liquor.
It's a fad, wouldn't you agree?

Life's a fad
Conceptualize nymphomania:
Compulsive sexual
Desire in women.

Life's a fad
Revisit misogyny:
Compulsive dislike for women.
What think you about that?

Life's a fad
Think of misogamy:
Compulsive aversion for marriage.
Any thoughts on that?

Life's a fad
Think of misanthropy:
Compulsive hatred of
Human-kind.

Truly
This life of ours
Is nothing but a huge farce!
What's your personal fads?

Tale of Two Nations

Call off the bluff!
There's no lost love between
Black and White in
Juneteenth Uncle Sam.
Not to the best of my knowledge.

A keen observer would
Testify that this country
Harbors two nations in one—
The one Caucasian;
The other Colored.

Black and white in love?
The color bar is palpable everywhere—
In all the nooks and crannies—
In the workplace;
In houses of worship.

Racism is omnipresent—
In shopping malls;
In communities of learners;
In eating houses;
In places of recreation.

Everywhere black and white behave like roadside
Strangers seeking shelter
From rain in an unknown place.
Each one waiting uncomfortably for the rain to cease.
So they can go their separate ways.
They barely tolerate one another.

Pseudo-Spouses

The notion of an ideal
Spouse sure is utopia.
At the same time,
Some spouses are
Plainly pseudo-spouses.

A henpecking spouse is no spouse.
He's a pseudo-spouse,
Notorious for tyranny and sulkiness.
A flirtatious spouse is no spouse.
He's a pseudo-spouse.

Notorious for cuckoldry.
A nagging wife is no wife.
She's like a sore tooth.
That keeps you awake all night.
Licking your bridal wounds.

A concubine is no wife.
She's a bird of passage,
Ready to take off
When the coast is dark.
She's a fair weather spouse.

One thing for sure,
When all is said and done,
A pseudo-spouse
Barring all flaws,
Is better than no spouse at all!

Nuptials

His siblings
Were stunned when he
Brought home an ex-whore for wife!

Even his old mother said:
The entire village will scoff at you
When you go by hand in hand.

Take time to know her,
It is not an overnight thing,
Eschew the "if" thing.

Little did she know that the
Infamous wedding would be the very
Undoing of her industrious son.

His untimely demise was
The end point of the machinations
Orchestrated by the fiendish woman he espoused.

Had he known,
Always the sobriquet
For Mr. Late.

Death Tracks

Ours are not roads.
They are booby-traps!
Oftentimes, commuters
are stuck in knee-deep mire,
pulling, pushing and digging.
Overwhelmed by frustration,
they curse, swear and pray
for divine assistance.

More often than not,
unloading the car,
improvising stones for wedges
is the only choice left
for desperate passengers.
Quite often,
the toil is futile.

This vicious cycle
will never end.
Generations before have trod
these death traps.
Today is our turn;
tomorrow will be
the turn of generations
yet to be born.

Prima Donnas

It's amazing how
Many small fries take
Themselves for big fishes.
I think that's because
They are impostors.

It's astonishing how
Many nitwits pass for gurus.
I think it's because
They are hell bent on fooling themselves.
They don't know any better.

It's perplexing how
Many average minds
Masquerade as super-stars.
I think it's because
They are half-baked.

It's unbelievable how
Many weaklings impersonate
As omnipotent beings.
I think it's because
They lack spines.

It's incredible how
Many indigent people
Want to be seen as clones
Of Warren Buffet; I think it's because
They are not honest to themselves.

If this world of ours
Were devoid of prima donnas
There would be no room for growth
This is time-tested truth.
Always room for improvement!

Heresy

In the beginning
God created the world
And populated it with
Good-natured humans.
And after a time,
He looked down and said:
Heavens! This place
Should be a zoo
So he created dictators.

On the second day,
He looked down again and said:
Gee! This place should be a circus.
So he created politicians.
On the third day,
He looked down again and said:
Goodness! This place should be
Kingdom of the occult.
So he created witches, wizards and soothsayers.

On the fourth day,
He looked down again and said:
Gracious! This place should
Be a vampire-dom.
So he created bloodsuckers.
On the fifth day, He looked down and said:
Heck! This place should be a whorehouse.
So he created harlots,
Lesbians, gays and pedophiles.

On the sixth day,
He looked down and said:
Hell! This place should be a war zone.
So he created terrorists
And warmongers.
On the seventh day,
God had finished His work.
He rested and called His creation
Human Zoo!

Three D's

I can't think of any canker
Eating into the moral fabric
Of our nation deeper than
The three D's: Drugs, Drinking, Divorce.

It's a horror to
Fathom kids in their teens
Consuming cocaine, heroin, LSD
And dagga[23] with impunity!

It's an eyesore to
See youngsters stinking like breweries.
Ours is a nation of dipsomaniacs!
This is the land of freedoms.

It's disheartening to
See the family edifice fall apart.
A nation that ignores the quintessence of
The family bond is an elephant with clay legs.

---

[23] marijuana

Ostrich

I'm an ostrich--
Large swift-running bird.
In the face of imminent danger,
I bury my head in the sand.

I'm an ostrich.
Kids indulge in debauchery,
I bury my head in the sand.
I feign to not see it.

I'm an ostrich.
Elected officials abuse public
Office with impunity.
I bury my head in the sand.

I'm an ostrich.
Divorce is rocking
The very foundation of our nation.
I bury my head in the sand.
I feign not seeing.

I am an ostrich
Legalized abortion has
Made us a murderous nation.
I bury my head in the sand.

I am an ostrich
Bogus marriages abound in our land.
I bury my head in the sand.
I feign to not see.

I'm an ostrich
Schools are a travesty of places of learning.
I bury my head in the sand.
I feign to not see.

I'm an ostrich
Church leaders are
Sanctimonious hypocrites.
I bury my head in the sand.

I'm who I am.
I abhor calling a spade a spade.
I love make-believe.
I'm an ostrich.

Cobweb

A cobweb is a network
Of threads spun by a spider
From secreted liquid.
It's a trap for insects,
An insidious entanglement
For unwary human beings.

Some folks go through school,
But school doesn't go through them at all.
The reason is because
They're entangled in a cobweb.
A great many folks look but don't see .
The reason is because they inhabit a cobweb.

Many more listen but don't hear.
The reason is because
They're entangled in a cobweb.
Others appear physically grown,
But remain mentally immature.
The reason is because they live in a cobweb.

A myriad more travel far and wide,
But internalize nothing from travels.
The reason is because they're in a cobweb.
Several folks talk the talk but don't walk the walk
The reason is they're buried in a cobweb.
Too many attend worship services but don't know God.

Guts

I hate the stinking guts
Of saucy ignoramuses.
Pride goes before a fall!

I hate the stinking guts
of these freaking fibsters.
They're living and partly living!

I hate the guts
Of cocky brats who talk back to elders.
They lack parental nurture.

I hate the bashful guts
Of religious fanatics.
They're servants of Satan!

I hate the silly guts
Of rapists and ilk
Real men don't rape!

I hate the f…king guts
Of sodomizers.
They're violators of the written law!

I hate the bloody guts
Of oligarchists.
Power corrupts; absolute corrupts absolutely!

I hate the maddening guts
Of misogynists.
Bigotry begets prejudice!

I hate the daredevil guts
Of misanthropists.
Hatred is a boomerang.

Causes Célèbres

Makes me laugh
To see Lilliputians
Parading themselves as
Alpha and omega of the universe.
That's self-delusion.

Makes me chuckle
To see little upstarts
Flaunting ill-gotten wealth.
That's like pulling wool
Over the eyes of folks.

Makes me crack up
To see natives shun their
Indigenous cultures and mores,
All in the name of fitting in!
That's self-denial.

Makes me laugh up my sleeve
To see half-baked individuals
Showing off as seasoned scholars.
That's like running against the wind.
That's tomfoolery at its best.

Makes me giggle
To see people confusing
Mundane wealth with rich spirituality.
That's living in fool's paradise.
We need to get our priorities right.

Makes me grin
To see mortals playing God.
The folly of humans is gargantuan!
These phony celebrities
Are indeed small fries.

Nudity

What we do today has the
Potential of being replicated tomorrow.
The dress code at school is a case in point.
Take a tour of schools in the vicinity.
You'd find a sizeable number of students
Gallivanting like peacocks semi-nude, pants hanging
Down precariously from their semi-nude butts!

Teachers and school administrators
Ought to have zero tolerance for such
Acts of impropriety
Well-groomed kids make a decent society.
Parents and Teachers
Have gotten more than their fair share of work to do.
Let's be mindful of that.

Pedagogue

Oh my teacher!
My dear teacher,
Sweet as honey,
Bright like the sun.
My loving teacher,
Your presence in class keeps me awake.

Oh my dear teacher!
You move hither and thither in class,
Hot in your desire to impart knowledge.
Oh my passionate teacher!
You don't give me a fish;
You teach me how to fish.

Oh my dear teacher!
What a blessing you are for me!
I hope I shall one day be like you.
Your ideas are tonic to my soul.
Your attire is a dress code.
Your words louder than they sound.

Wow, my dear teacher!
How great art thou,
You are a role-model,
Knowledgeable, personable,
Passionate and assiduous—
A great nation builder.

Graffiti

Graffiti
Have you ever read obscene graffiti?
The more I read graffiti,
The more I think about its
Nefarious effect on our collective psyche.
Ponder this one culled from a men's
Restroom in one of the nation's colleges:

"Can you suck my dick?
Are you just a bunch of fags who could
Never get their cocks wet unless
They are dropping roofie[24] in girls' drinks?
You should all get fucking lives, or
Get the fuck out of here!"
Speaks volumes. Doesn't it?

---

[24] Sedative often used as a date-rape drug

Red Lights

In this fast train
Where we are:
Teenagers falling pregnant,
We need red lights to halt the insanity.

In this top-speed train
Where we are:
Underage kids wielding firearms,
We need red lights to stop the lunacy.

In this breakneck train
Where we are:
School kids peddling drugs,
We need red lights to halt the dementia.

In this maddening train
Where we are:
Minors consuming liquor with no qualms,
We need red lights to stop the madness.

In this high-speed train
Where we are:
Young mothers dumping newborns in trashcans,
We need red lights to halt the derangement.

Color Blind

Human beings come in all shapes and colors.
We must recognize and nurture them all
Without racialist or xenophobic feelings.
God's garden is multicolored for a reason…

We are all so different,
In the most part because we
Are all endowed with different
Combinations of pigmentation…

I nurse the conviction that we would
A have better world to live in,
If only we would take advantage of our
Innate differences and multiple intelligences.

Diaper

Did you know?
That a bossy boss is like a diaper:
Always in your ass,
And often full of shit!

Did you know?
A nagging spouse is like a diaper:
Always in your ass.
And often full of caca![25]

Did you know?
A dependent sibling is like a diaper:
Always in your ass,
And often full of bullshit!

Did you know?
A prodigal son is like a diaper:
Always in your ass,
And often full of crap!

Did you know?
A gossiping neighbor is like a diaper:
Always in your ass-hole,
And often full of poop!

---

[25] Shit in French

Kokombioko Intellectuals

Ponder this irony of sorts—
An impressive number of self-styled
Academics are indeed uneducated,
Highly certificated and yet unschooled.

How can one flaunt a string
Of degrees and yet comport oneself
In the most uncouth manner imaginable?
Highly certificated and yet uneducated.

Pseudo-intellectuals are blokes
Who have passed through schools,
Yet school has not passed through them.
They're kokombioko [26]intellos[27]

Conventional wisdom ordains
That a disciplined mind be couth at all times.
To be educated is tantamount
To being a role-model.

---

[26] Mushroom
[27] Intellectuals

Rainbow

Oftentimes, I marvel at the
Imbecility characteristic of racial bigots.
Is a black dog less serviceable
To its master than a white dog?
So, why are we bent on using
Color bar as a rod for
Calibrating human potential?

I am astounded by the inanity
Of disciples of Jim Crow.
Is a red flower worthier
Than a purple flower?
So, why do we insist on
Compartmentalizing the
World along color lines?

I am dumbfounded by the
Hollowness typical of the skewed
Reasoning of racist pigs.
Is a brown grass-hopper any less valuable
Than a pink grass-hopper?
So, why do we continue to use
Skin color as a test of human prowess?

I am horrified at the
Idiocy of the apostles of apartheid.
Is a blue sparrow more important
Than a brown sparrow?
So, why do we continue to put
A premium on color differences?
There's the question!

Tokenism

In this day and age
When men are led by toys—
Oscars, Grammies, Medals, Medallions,
And countless other status symbols,
We need to step back and interrogate
Ourselves on the raison d'être of these trophies.

It is written:
Whosoever wants to save his life will lose it.
What good will it be for a man
If he gains the entire universe yet loses his life?
Scriptures teach us to shun mundane stuff
And lead selfless and righteous lives.

Fool's Paradise

Pipe Dream

Isn't it funny that some folks
Believe that humans can become
Crocodiles by simply lying in water?
If wishes were horses,
Beggars would ride!

Isn't it ludicrous that some people
Hold onto the idea that one can become a car
By just sitting in the garage?
If wishes were horses,
Beggars would ride!

Isn't it self-delusion to
Believe that pitching up in church
Every Sunday is a ticket into Paradise?
If wishes were horses,
Beggars would ride!

Gosh!

Our decadent culture,
One that eschews moral etiquettes.
Such is our culture,
One that places the "me" credo
At the epicenter of social intercourse.

In our decadent culture,
Reference to God is anathema.
In the name of political correctness,
"God" has metamorphosed into "Gosh."
God is on exile. My Gosh!

Such is our culture,
Kids have a whimsical attitude toward sex
Something you do with a guy for fun.
Divorce has skyrocketed,
Abortion is the norm. My Gosh!

Erosion of moral values
Is wreaking irreparable havoc
On the social fiber
And on public and private lives.
My Gosh!

Malapropism

To some, the way he walks
And talks is the body language
Of courage and self-assurance.
To others he's a punk ass chump.
I mean a scumbag.

It's the swagger and smirk
That signal the certainty of a simpleton.
He comes across as a nincompoop,
Though technically he's not a numskull.
 But he could pass for a scallywag.

He is a roving time bomb
When you stop to think
About his political antics.
The rank and file like him,
But loathe his policies.

His malapropisms
And mangled syntax
Have given late-night comedians
As much fodder for cannon
As his predecessor's lustful lifestyle.

People are sick and tired
Of a leader who believes
That he's leading through
A higher power alien from reality.
That's hogwash!

Despite coming into office
Without a mandate,
He has ruled as if he had one.
He's a conviction politician
Who doesn't care a hoot what he knows not.

Guinea Pigs

Man has waged many
A war against man
Since the dawn of history.
But the mother of all wars
Is the genetic warfare.

Genetics no longer
Symbolizes merely
Molecules of DNA.
It connotes war-mongering.
In the hands of villains.

Inorganic substances
Have made the concept of longevity
A laughing stock
Ponder the anthrax scare,
The pandemonium it engendered.

Gene-tech is the root
Of a good many ills—
Disruptor of the ecosystem,
Emasculator of biodiversity,
Harbinger of soil and water pollution.

No one is sure of the
Long-term effects of
Genetic engineering
On the physical and
Human environments.

The more we speculate,
The more illusory it becomes.
Consider the specter of cloned
Environmental terrorists!
Aren't we all guinea pigs?

Imbroglio

I wear the shoe,
So I know where it pinches.
Talk of racism to a man who
Has never been bitten
He'd scoff at you.

June 6th, 2001 was D-day.
Date of the Yearbook imbroglio.
On that day it dawned on me
That my name and photo
Had been omitted from the Yearbook.

Some thingamabob had deemed it
Necessary to whitewash the Yearbook
By obliterating the lone black face.
Madison Middle School Yearbook--
Creation of racial bigots!

After a whole academic year of toil
One would have expected
Hugs and gestures of gratitude from and peers.
Conversely, a certain Ms. Sara had
Deemed it proper to reward my hard work with scorn.

It all goes to prove a point—
Man is born free but everywhere in chains—
Chains of bigotry;
Shackles of myopia;
Fetters of backwoods mentality.

Locked Horns

Debunk the conspiracy theory!
The tragedy was no fortuitous event,
But rather a coordinated operation
Masterminded within their borders!

The raison d'être of the op?
The birth of a Euro-Asian alliance
Via an artificial clash of values—
The Alterity imbrioglio.

The Al-Queda hullabaloo
Some window-dressing
To veil our grand-style strategic agenda.
Media propagandists being the dogs of wars.

In God's Name We Swear

I swear we believe in
God the Father,
God the Son
And God the Ghost.

We believe in,
Man's inalienable right to life,
Even if we legalize abortion.
That's because Lucifer ordained it.

Our believe in the sanctity of human life
Does not deter us from vetting
The death penalty.
That's because Lucifer ordained it.

We believe,
In equality before the law
Even if we live in a caste system
That's because Lucifer ordained it.

We believe in public decency
Even if our right to consume pornography
Is enshrined in our Constitution
That's because Lucifer ordained it.

We believe in moral rectitude,
Even if we give leeway
To queer modus vivendi.
That's because Lucifer ordained it.

We believe in the right to life

Even if we aid and abet
Firearm proliferation.
That's because Lucifer ordained it.

We believe that substance abuse is
The bane of our society,
Even if we turn a blind eye to drug peddling.
That's because Lucifer ordained it.

We believe that promiscuity is evil,
Even if we do nothing to stop
Multiple sexual partnerships
That's because Lucifer ordained it.

See, man proposes
But God disposes.
Willy Nilly,
In God we distrust.

Sophism

Proponents of capital punishment
Believe that the death penalty
Is a panacea for odious criminality.

Opponents contend that
Race, politics, geography and money
Determine who is on death-roll.

Capital punishment is costly.
The price of capital punishment
Is the cost of giving up the ideals of humanity.

The question of erroneous executions
Makes capital punishment untenable.
The deterrence argument is not cogent either.

The racial factor in capital punishment
Debunks the myth of
Equal justice under the law.

The big lie about painless execution
Is a fad that's devoid of meaning.
There's nothing painless about legal homicide.

Nirvana

Heaven is a place of external bliss
It is a place of great joy.
In Heaven there will be no
More pain or sorrow.
In Heaven there will be no
More illness or death.
It'll be a place of eternal glee—
The Nirvana…

There's one question
We must ask ourselves—
If we died today,
Where would we go?
Would our souls enter Heaven or Hell?
And if we got to Heaven,
Why would God permit us to stay there?
Do we really belong in Nirvana?

Social Contract

The social contract—bond of social intercourse.
Civil society presumes rational comportment.
Human civilizations have established
Governments by which they run civil societies.

Nonetheless, there's need to assume
Machiavellian conduct—
Deceit and irrationality--
On the part of bureaucrats.

Pursuit of self-interest,
More often than not is
Veiled in self-perception of altruism,
Smoke-screen self-service.

Irrational behavior emanating
From the powers-that-be
Constitutes a breach of the social contract—
With the attendant result of organized chaos.

Pursuit of Happiness

Root cause of unhappiness
Is the insatiable quest for stuff.
Belief that happiness stems from
Getting all that we want is a fallacy.
Truth of the matter is that our desire to own
More than we really need engenders unhappiness.

The sure route to happiness
Is to seek stuff that inspires true happiness.
If we place our hearts solely on possessions,
The end result will be moroseness.
More often than not we desire things that ruin us.
Let's resist the temptation of sinking into materialism.

Soul-Searching

Sure, you've heard.
God created man and woman
And from dust made them partners.

For this reason
A man shall leave his father
And mother and cleave to his wife.

And, the two shall become one in flesh.
What God has put together.
Let no man put asunder.

So, is same sex matrimony
A human aberration
Or flaw in divine creative genius?

Double-Speak

Our penchant for
Convoluted lingo is notorious.
To make the ordinary
Seem extraordinary.

Auto-mechanics
Have known a re-rebirth--
They've become
Automotive internists.

Elevator operators pass for
Vertical transportation corps.
Double-speak is the stock-in-trade
Of the man-of-war.

Pre-emptive counter-attack
Veils our inborn belligerence.
Tactical redeployment is the
Euphemism for military retreat.

The War dubbed
An incursion fails to
Qualify for an invasion.
We no longer talk of bullet holes—

They're ballistics induced
Apertures in the subcutaneous
Firmament of the natural environment.
That's pretty smart!

Our neutron bombs

Have metamorphosed into
Radiation enhancement devices.
Such double-speak breeds fire-power.

No Child Left Behind

Being the teacher that I am,
It's my constitutional right
To have my say on the
No Child Left Behind[28] fad.

I wonder why the
No Child Left Behind
Modus operandi isn't applicable
To other forms of business.

I have thought about the
Plummeting cost of eggs
And wondered why testing chickens
Wouldn't be effective in raising egg prices.

The powers-that-be should
Be thinking of mandating the
Testing of all chickens each year.
I know full well that it will take time off

Poultry man's daily schedule
To accomplish this herculean task.
It may even require spending
Astronomical sums of money

On the purchase of testing equipment.
But this is what it takes

---

[28] The *No Child Left Behind Act* is a United States Act of Congress that is a reauthorization of the Elementary and Secondary Education Act, which included Title I, the government's flagship aid program for disadvantaged students. The legislation was proposed by President George W. Bush on January 23, 2001.

To get the onerous task done.

We will have to determine
Which chickens fully meet the standard,
Which ones barely meet the standard,
Which ones meet the standard with honors

And which show evidence of underachievement.
Points will be assigned.
It will be necessary for each
Category to achieve a given average score.

Otherwise, the Department of Agriculture
Will either send experts to give advice
Or simply take over the poultry.
No kidding at all!

It is noteworthy that every chicken
Can meet set standards.
So there's no room for excuses!
There aren't going to be any exceptions.

All chickens must meet the standards set
By the powers-that-be in the ivory towel poultry farm.
Every poultry will be placed
In the care of a certified poultry man.

There will be poultry choice for chickens.
Underachieving chickens will be
Allowed to move to poultry of their choice.
This will force under-performing poultries to buckle up

Some poultries may be forced to
Wind up on account of this new law.
That's regrettable but taxpayers cannot
Continue to subsidize underachieving poultries!

Suicide Mission

I see a group of compatriots,
Black man and white man,
Headed for a suicide mission on the war front.

I see a bunch of corporate rogues,
Black man and white man,
Bent on despoiling alien lands.

I see countless numbers of
Hapless sons and daughters of our land,
Serving as fodder for cannon!

How long shall we continue to pull
The wool over the eyes of citizens,
Day and Night, come sun come rain?

How long shall we endeavor
To hoodwink denizens into believing,
That our belligerence serves their interest?

Printed in the United States
By Bookmasters